101 SOUPS, SALADS & SANDWICHES

Skillet–Toasted Corn Salad, page 44

Green Pepper Soup, page 9

Grilled Chicken & Zucchini Wraps, page 74

Gooseberry Patch
2500 Farmers Dr., #110
Columbus, OH 43235

www.gooseberrypatch.com
1·800·854·6673

Gooseberry Patch *cookbooks*

Since 1992, we've been publishing our own country cookbooks for every kitchen and for every meal of the day! Each title has hundreds of budget-friendly recipes, using ingredients you already have on hand in your pantry.

In addition, you'll find helpful tips and ideas on every page, along with our hand-drawn artwork and plenty of personality. Their lay-flat binding makes them so easy to use...they're sure to become a fast favorite in your kitchen.

Fruit Harvest Salad,
page 52

Creamy Chicken & Wild Rice Soup, page 18

Call us toll-free at
1•800•854•6673
and we'd be delighted to tell you all about our newest titles!

Shop with us online anytime at
www.gooseberrypatch.com

Send us your favorite recipe!

and the memory that makes it special for you!* If we select your recipe for a brand-new **Gooseberry Patch** cookbook, your name will appear right along with it...and you'll receive a FREE copy of the book!

Submit your recipe on our website at
www.gooseberrypatch.com

Or mail to:

Gooseberry Patch • Attn: Cookbook Dept.
2500 Farmers Dr., #110 • Columbus, OH 43235

*Please include the number of servings and all other necessary information!

Have a taste for more?

Visit **www.gooseberrypatch.com** to join our **Circle of Friends**!

- Free recipes, tips and ideas plus a complete cookbook index
- Get special email offers and our monthly eLetter delivered to your inbox
- Find local stores with **Gooseberry Patch** cookbooks, calendars and organizers

Toasted Chicken Salad Bagels, page 85

Bacon-Onion Croutons, page 99

Chicken & Dumplin' Soup, page 11

Asian Summer Salad, page 39

Chicken Tacos, page 87

Creamy Basil Salad Dressing, page 100

White Bean & Tomato Salad, page 47

CONTENTS

Meatball Vegetable Cheese Soup, page 13

Dedication

To everyone who
likes satisfying recipes
from lunchtime to
dinnertime and
every time in between!

Appreciation

To cooks everywhere
who sent us their
best-tasting recipes…
thank you!

Texas Steak Sandwiches, page 82

Spicy Sausage Chowder

16-oz. pkg. sweet Italian pork
   sausage links, diced
1 onion, finely chopped
2 cloves garlic, minced
15-oz. can diced tomatoes
4-oz. can chopped green chiles
15-1/4 oz. can corn
14-1/2 oz. can chicken broth
8-oz. jar enchilada sauce
1 t. dried oregano
1 t. chili powder
1 t. salt
1 t. pepper
2 c. water

In a skillet over medium heat, cook
sausage until golden; drain. In a
slow cooker, stir in sausage and
remaining ingredients. Cover and
cook on low setting for 6 to 8 hours,
or on high setting for 3 to 4 hours.
Serve with Tortilla Crisps. Serves 4
to 6.

Tortilla Crisps:

4 whole-wheat tortillas
olive oil

Lightly brush both sides of tortillas
with olive oil. Cut into wedges. Bake
at 400 degrees on an ungreased
baking sheet for 8 to 10 minutes,
until crisp.

7

Sarah Gardner
Clifton Park, NY

This easy recipe has become
a staple in our household
during the holidays. Just
add all ingredients to the
slow cooker and leave it
to work its magic!

Chicken Noodle Gumbo

2 lbs. boneless, skinless chicken
   breasts, cut into 1-inch cubes
4 16-oz. cans chicken broth
15-oz. can diced tomatoes
32-oz. pkg. frozen okra, corn,
   celery and red pepper mixed
   vegetables
8-oz. pkg. bowtie pasta, uncooked
1/2 t. garlic powder
salt and pepper to taste

Place chicken, broth and tomatoes in
a large soup pot. Bring to a boil over
medium heat. Reduce heat; simmer
10 minutes. Add frozen vegetables,
uncooked pasta and seasonings. Return
to a boil. Cover and simmer one hour.
Serves 8 to 10.

Lorrie Smith
Drummonds, TN

This colorful dish makes
enough to feed a whole bunch
of hungry folks! Look for the
"gumbo blend" of frozen
vegetables at the market.

Green Pepper Soup

2 lbs. ground beef
28-oz. can tomato sauce
28-oz. can diced tomatoes
2 c. cooked rice
2 c. green peppers, chopped
2 cubes beef bouillon
1/4 c. brown sugar, packed
2 t. pepper

In a stockpot over medium heat, brown beef; drain. Add remaining ingredients and bring to a boil. Reduce heat; cover and simmer for 30 to 40 minutes, until peppers are tender. Makes 8 to 10 servings.

9

Sharon Laney
Mogadore, OH

Fall brings thoughts of a bountiful harvest with gardens and roadside stands overflowing with fresh vegetables...and this hearty soup.

Kielbasa Soup

1 head cabbage, shredded
16-oz. pkg. Kielbasa sausage, sliced
2 16-oz. cans diced tomatoes
1 onion, chopped
2 zucchini, quartered and sliced
2 yellow squash, quartered and
    sliced
2 T. seasoned salt
2 cloves garlic, crushed
1 cube beef bouillon
1 t. dried oregano
2 redskin or russet potatoes, cubed

In a stockpot, combine all ingredients
except potatoes. Cover ingredients with
water; bring to a boil. Cover, reduce
heat and simmer for 1-1/2 to 2 hours.
Add potatoes during last 30 minutes of
cook time. Makes 8 to 10 servings.

Pamela Bennett
Whittier, CA

My mom made up this recipe
one evening when there
wasn't a lot to eat in the
house. It has since become
a favorite comfort food!

Chicken & Dumplin' Soup

10-3/4 oz. can cream of chicken
   soup
4 c. chicken broth
4 boneless, skinless chicken
   breasts, cooked and shredded
2 15-oz. cans mixed vegetables
2 12-oz. tubes refrigerated
   biscuits, quartered

Bring soup and broth to a slow boil
in a saucepan over medium heat;
whisk until smooth. Stir in chicken
and vegetables; bring to a boil. Drop
biscuit quarters into soup; cover and
simmer for 15 minutes. Remove
from heat. Let stand 10 minutes
before serving. Serves 4 to 6.

11

Brenda Hancock
Hartford, NY
This is truly comfort food at
its finest. And with the help
of refrigerated biscuits, it
couldn't be easier!

Surprise Bean Soup

16-oz. pkg. bacon, cut into
   1-inch pieces
1 onion, chopped
1 c. carrot, peeled and diced
1 c. celery, chopped
15-oz. can tomato sauce
15-oz. can diced tomatoes
1 c. chicken broth
2 15-oz. cans navy beans, drained
3/4 c. creamy peanut butter
1/2 t. pepper

In a skillet over medium heat, cook
bacon until crisp; drain. Return bacon
to skillet; stir in onion, carrot and
celery, cooking until onion is
translucent. In a large stockpot over
medium heat, stir together bacon
mixture, tomato sauce, diced tomatoes,
chicken broth and beans until hot and
bubbly. Stir in peanut butter and
pepper until well combined. Serve
immediately. Makes 6 servings.

Susan Jacobs
Vista, CA

My hubby took my bean soup
recipe and added his favorite
ingredient...peanut butter!

Meatball-Vegetable Cheese Soup

1 lb. ground beef
1/4 c. dry bread crumbs
1 egg, beaten
1/2 t. salt
1/2 t. hot pepper sauce
1 c. celery, chopped
1/2 c. onion, chopped
2 cubes beef bouillon
1 c. corn
1 c. potato, peeled and diced
1/2 c. carrot, peeled and sliced
2 c. water
16-oz. jar pasteurized process
    cheese sauce

In a bowl, mix together beef, bread crumbs, egg, salt and hot sauce; form into one-inch balls. Place in a slow cooker. Add remaining ingredients except cheese sauce. Cover and cook on low setting for 8 to 10 hours. Immediately before serving, stir in cheese sauce until combined. Cover and cook an additional 10 minutes, until warmed through. Serves 6.

13

Denise Webb
Galveston, IN

You'll want to try this
slow-cooker recipe...it's
a real family-pleaser!

Cream of Zucchini Soup

3 lbs. zucchini, sliced
   1/2-inch thick
2 onions, quartered
5 slices bacon
4 c. chicken broth
1 t. salt
1 t. pepper
Optional: 1/2 t. garlic powder
Garnish: onion and garlic
   croutons, or butter and grated
   Parmesan cheese

Combine all ingredients except garnish
in a soup pot over medium heat. Cook
until zucchini is tender and bacon is
cooked, about 45 minutes. Ladle soup
into a blender and process until
smooth. Return to soup pot; heat
through. Serve topped with croutons or
with a pat of butter and a sprinkling of
Parmesan cheese. Makes 6 servings.

Susan Maurer
Dahlgren, IL

One taste and you'll
agree...there's really
no such thing as too
many zucchini!

Chilled Melon Soup

3 c. cantaloupe melon, peeled,
   seeded and chopped
2 T. sugar, divided
1/4 c. orange juice, divided
1/8 t. salt, divided
3 c. honeydew melon, peeled,
   seeded and chopped
Garnish: fresh mint sprigs or
   orange slices

In a blender, process cantaloupe, half the sugar, half the juice and half the salt until smooth. Cover and refrigerate. Repeat with honeydew and remaining ingredients except garnish. Refrigerate, covered, in separate containers. To serve, pour equal amounts of each mixture at the same time on opposite sides of individual soup bowls. Garnish as desired. Makes 4 to 6 servings.

15

Janice Woods
Northern Cambria, PA
This tasty and beautiful recipe is perfect for summer get-togethers with friends.

Pepper Jack-Crab Bisque

2 T. butter
2 stalks celery, finely chopped
1 onion, finely chopped
2 10-3/4 oz. cans tomato bisque
  or tomato soup
2-1/2 c. whipping cream or
  half-and-half
3 8-oz. pkgs. imitation crabmeat,
  flaked
1-1/2 c. shredded Pepper Jack
  cheese

Melt butter in a stockpot over medium heat. Add celery and onion; cook until softened. Add bisque or soup, cream or half-and-half and crabmeat. Simmer over low heat until heated through; stir in cheese. If too thick, add a little more cream or half-and-half as desired. Makes 6 servings.

Wendy Ball
Battle Creek, MI
My husband and I had enjoyed a soup like this when dining out with our good friends, Rick and Carolyn. My efforts to recreate it really paid off...we love it!

Beef Stew & Biscuits

1 lb. ground beef
1/4 c. onion, chopped
1/4 t. dried basil
1/8 t. pepper
3-1/2 c. frozen or canned mixed
   vegetables
2 8-oz. cans tomato sauce
1 c. sharp Cheddar cheese, cubed
12-oz. tube refrigerated biscuits

In a skillet, brown beef and onion;
drain. Add seasonings, mixed
vegetables and tomato sauce; mix
well. Cover and simmer for
5 minutes. Fold in cheese cubes;
pour into an ungreased 2-quart
casserole dish. Arrange biscuits on
top. Bake, uncovered, at 375 degrees
for 25 minutes, or until biscuits are
golden. Serves 4 to 6.

Jocelyn Medina
Phoenixville, PA
This tried & true one-pot
meal is perfect for
Sunday dinner.

Creamy Chicken & Wild Rice Soup

4 boneless, skinless chicken
  breasts, cubed
3/4 lb. carrot, peeled and sliced
3 stalks celery, sliced
1 onion, diced
2 4.3-oz. pkgs. long-grain and
  wild rice mix
4 10-3/4 oz. cans cream of potato
  soup
32-oz. container chicken broth
2 c. whipping cream

In a slow cooker, layer chicken, carrot,
celery, onion, rice with seasoning
packets and potato soup. Pour broth
over top. Cover and cook on low
setting for 8 hours. Stir thoroughly.
Mix in cream; cover and heat through,
about 15 minutes. Serves 8 to 10.

Patty Habig Bowen
Westfield, NY

I've tweaked this slow-cooker
recipe so many times, it's
nothing like the original!
It's so thick, you can
use the leftovers for
chicken pot pie filling.

Fred's Chunky Chili

1 lb. ground beef or turkey,
   browned and drained
3/4 c. green pepper, diced
1 t. garlic, minced
3/4 c. onion, diced
6-oz. can tomato paste
14-1/2 oz. can stewed tomatoes
15-1/2 oz. can kidney beans
1/4 c. salsa
1 T. sugar
1/2 t. cayenne pepper
1/2 t. dried cilantro
1 t. dried basil
Garnish: shredded Cheddar
   cheese, crackers

19

Combine all ingredients except
garnish in a Dutch oven. Bring to
a simmer over medium-high heat.
Cover and simmer over low heat for
30 minutes, stirring occasionally.
Serve with cheese and crackers.
Serves 4 to 6.

Marian Muder
Hubbard, OH

My husband has been
making his signature chili
for years now. It's a
combination of several
tasty recipes.

Pioneer Beef Stew

14-1/2 oz. can petite diced
   tomatoes
1 c. water
3 T. quick-cooking tapioca,
   uncooked
2 t. sugar
1-1/2 t. salt
1/2 t. pepper
1-1/2 lbs. stew beef, cubed
3 to 4 potatoes, peeled and cubed
4 carrots, peeled and thickly sliced
1 onion, diced

In a large bowl, combine tomatoes with juice, water, tapioca, sugar, salt and pepper. Mix well; stir in remaining ingredients. Pour into a greased 3-quart casserole dish. Cover and bake at 375 degrees for 1-1/2 to 2 hours, until beef and vegetables are tender. Serves 4 to 6.

Angie O'Keefe
Soddy Daisy, TN

There's nothing more satisfying than a hearty bowl of beef stew! It's baked, not simmered on the stovetop...no need to watch it.

Macaroni & Cheese Chowder

14-oz. can chicken broth
1 c. water
1 c. elbow macaroni, uncooked
1 c. milk
8-oz. pkg. pasteurized process
    cheese spread
1 c. cooked ham, diced
1 c. corn

Over medium heat, bring broth and
water to a boil in a saucepan. Add
macaroni and cook until tender,
about 12 minutes. Reduce heat to
low. Add milk, cheese, ham and
corn. Simmer and stir until cheese
is melted. Serves 4 to 6.

21

Alissa Sellers
Bangor, PA

This recipe is a family
favorite that even my young
son loves! It's perfect for
a quick family dinner,
especially on a cold
or rainy night.

Chill-Chaser Pork Stew

2 to 2-1/2 lbs. pork steaks, cubed
2 T. olive oil
2 sweet onions, chopped
2 green peppers, chopped
2 cloves garlic, minced
salt and pepper to taste
6-oz. can tomato paste
28-oz. can diced tomatoes
2 8-oz. cans sliced mushrooms,
  drained

In a Dutch oven over medium heat, sauté pork in oil until browned. Add onions, green peppers, garlic, salt and pepper. Cover; cook over medium heat until pork is tender. Add tomato paste, tomatoes with juice and mushrooms; bring to a boil. Reduce heat to low; simmer for one hour, stirring often. Serves 6.

Kathy McCann-Neff
Claxton, GA

After a day of raking leaves, this stew warms and rejuvenates you!

Creamy Split Pea Soup

1 lb. bacon, crisply cooked,
    crumbled and 2 to 3 T.
    drippings reserved
1 onion, diced
2 stalks celery, diced
8 c. water
16-oz. pkg. dried split peas
2 potatoes, peeled and diced
2 t. salt
1/4 t. pepper
3 cubes beef bouillon
1 bay leaf
1 c. half-and-half

23

Heat reserved bacon drippings in a
large soup pot; sauté onion and
celery over medium heat until tender.
Add remaining ingredients except
half-and-half; bring to a boil over
medium-high heat. Reduce heat
to low; cover and simmer for
45 minutes, until peas are very
tender. Discard bay leaf. Fill a
blender 3/4 full with soup; blend
to purée. Return to soup pot; stir
in half-and-half. Simmer over
medium heat for 5 minutes, until
heated through. Garnish with
reserved bacon. Serves 8.

Kathy Schroeder
Vermilion, OH

This soup was a sensation
at my daughter's baby
shower...so much flavor!

Tomato-Ravioli Soup

1 lb. ground beef
28-oz. can crushed tomatoes
6-oz. can tomato paste
2 c. water
1-1/2 c. onion, chopped
2 cloves garlic, minced
1/4 c. fresh parsley, chopped
3/4 t. dried basil
1/2 t. dried oregano
1/4 t. dried thyme
1/2 t. onion salt
1/2 t. salt
1/4 t. pepper
1/2 t. sugar
9-oz. pkg. frozen cheese ravioli
1/4 c. grated Parmesan cheese

In a Dutch oven, cook beef over medium heat until no longer pink; drain. Stir in tomatoes with juice, tomato paste, water, onion, garlic, seasonings and sugar. Bring to a boil. Reduce heat; cover and simmer for 30 minutes. Meanwhile, cook ravioli as package directs; drain. Add ravioli to soup and heat through. Stir in Parmesan cheese; serve immediately. Makes 6 to 8 servings.

Heather Quinn
Gilmer, TX

This soup has a light, smooth flavor...there's always an empty pot afterwards!

Chicken Corn Chowder

1-1/2 c. milk
10-1/2 oz. can chicken broth
10-3/4 oz. can cream of chicken
    soup
10-3/4 oz. can cream of potato
    soup
1 to 2 10-oz. cans chicken,
    drained
1/3 c. green onion, chopped
11-oz. can sweet corn & diced
    peppers
4-oz. can chopped green chiles,
    drained
8-oz. pkg. shredded Cheddar
    cheese

25

Mix together all ingredients except cheese in a stockpot. Cook over low heat, stirring frequently, for 15 minutes, or until heated through. Add cheese; stir until melted. Serves 6 to 8.

Katie French
Portland, TX

A quick main dish that goes great with a big, buttery piece of cornbread.

Swiss Potato Soup

12 slices bacon, coarsely chopped
1 onion, chopped
4 green onions, coarsely chopped
6 c. cabbage, coarsely chopped
4 potatoes, peeled and diced
6 c. chicken broth
2 c. Gruyère cheese, shredded
1 c. light cream
1 T. dill weed
salt and pepper to taste

Sauté bacon in a large stockpot for
3 minutes. Drain, reserving
2 tablespoons drippings in skillet.
Add onions and cabbage; cook
5 minutes. Add potatoes and broth;
bring to a boil. Reduce heat and
simmer 40 minutes. Pour into a
blender, a little at a time, and blend
until smooth. Pour back into stockpot.
Add cheese gradually, stirring to melt.
Do not boil. Stir in remaining
ingredients just before serving.
Serves 6 to 8.

Vickie

Sometimes I'll replace the
green onions with two
leeks...scrumptious
either way!

Chicken Enchilada Soup

1 onion, chopped
1 clove garlic, pressed
1 to 2 t. oil
14-1/2 oz. can beef broth
14-1/2 oz. can chicken broth
10-3/4 oz. can cream of chicken
   soup
1-1/2 c. water
12-1/2 oz. can chicken, drained
4-oz. can chopped green chiles
2 t. Worcestershire sauce
1 T. steak sauce
1 t. ground cumin
1 t. chili powder
1/8 t. pepper
6 corn tortillas, cut into strips
1 c. shredded Cheddar cheese

In a stockpot over medium heat, sauté onion and garlic in oil. Add remaining ingredients except tortilla strips and cheese; bring to a boil. Cover; reduce heat and simmer for one hour, stirring occasionally. Uncover; stir in tortilla strips and cheese. Simmer an additional 10 minutes. Serves 6.

Jeanne Dinnel
Canby, OR

This recipe may look lengthy, but it goes together in a jiffy! Serve it with a simple salad of ripe tomato and avocado drizzled with lime vinaigrette dressing.

Chili Stew

1/2 onion, chopped
1/2 red pepper, chopped
1/2 yellow pepper, chopped
1 butternut squash, peeled
   and cubed
2 T. oil
1 T. garlic, chopped
1 lb. ground beef
1 T. smoked paprika
2 t. ground cumin
2 t. dried basil
2 t. dried thyme
1/8 to 1/4 t. Worcestershire sauce
28-oz. can plum tomatoes
28-oz. can diced tomatoes
15-1/2 oz. can kidney beans,
   drained and rinsed
15-1/2 oz. can black beans,
   drained and rinsed
2 T. all-purpose flour
2 c. beef broth
salt and pepper to taste

In a stockpot, cook onion, peppers and squash in oil until tender. Add garlic and beef. Cook until beef is browned; drain. Add spices, Worcestershire sauce, tomatoes and beans; break up tomatoes with a spoon. In a bowl, mix flour and broth; stir into chili. Bring to a boil. Reduce heat, cover and simmer for 30 minutes to 2 hours. Season with salt and pepper. Serves 6.

Linda Marshall
Ontario, Canada
I planned to make chili, only to discover that I had no chili powder. So I put this together instead, and now it's our favorite.

Clam & Scallop Chowder

2 onions, finely chopped
1/4 c. butter, divided
1 t. salt
1 t. pepper
1 c. chicken broth or water
2 potatoes, peeled and cubed
1/4 lb. bay scallops
10-oz. can baby clams, drained
    and 1/2 c. liquid reserved
1 c. light cream
1 c. milk
2 slices bacon, crisply cooked
    and crumbled

In a large heavy saucepan over medium heat, cook onions in 2 tablespoons butter for 5 minutes, or until tender. Add salt, pepper, broth or water and potatoes; cook until fork tender. Reduce heat; add scallops and cook just until tender, 4 to 5 minutes. Stir in clams with reserved liquid, cream, milk, bacon and remaining butter. Heat through without boiling for 3 minutes, or until hot. Serves 4.

Lisa Purcell
Ontario, Canada

For a special presentation, serve this steaming chowder in hollowed-out rounds of sourdough bread...oh-so good!

29

Kitchen Cabinet Mild White Chili

2 15-1/2 oz. cans great Northern
   beans
Optional: 4-1/2 oz. can diced
   green chiles
14-oz. can chicken broth
1 T. dried, minced onion
1 T. red pepper flakes
1-1/2 t. dried, minced garlic
1 t. ground cumin
1/2 t. dried oregano
1/8 t. cayenne pepper
1/8 t. ground cloves
1-1/2 c. cooked chicken, chopped
4-oz. can sliced mushrooms,
   drained
1 c. shredded sharp Cheddar
   cheese

In a Dutch oven, combine all
ingredients except chicken, mushrooms
and cheese. Cook over medium heat
for 5 minutes; bring to a boil. Reduce
heat and simmer 5 minutes. Add
chicken and mushrooms; simmer,
uncovered, for 8 to 10 minutes, until
heated through. Serve with cheese.
Makes 4 servings.

Becky Hall
Belton, MO

This recipe was created on a
cold night with ingredients
from the kitchen cabinet. It
can easily be spiced up with
a can of diced chiles or
chopped jalapeño peppers.

BBQ Sloppy Joe Soup

1 lb. ground beef chuck
16-oz. can barbecue Sloppy Joe
    sauce
10-3/4 oz. can cream of potato
    soup
10-3/4 oz. can minestrone soup
1-1/4 c. water
15-oz. can light red kidney
    beans, drained and rinsed
14-1/2 oz. can green beans,
    drained
15-1/4 oz. can green peas,
    drained
15-oz. can diced tomatoes,
    drained
garlic powder and steak
    seasoning to taste
Garnish: oyster crackers

31

In a large saucepan over medium heat, brown beef; drain. Stir in Sloppy Joe sauce; heat through. Add remaining ingredients except crackers; simmer until bubbly, about 10 to 15 minutes. Serve with crackers. Makes 6 to 8 servings.

Betty Lou Wright
Hendersonville, TN

This recipe was a happy accident! One day I made vegetable soup. Remembering leftover Sloppy Joe sauce in the fridge, I stirred it into the soup. What a hit!

Bean & Sausage Soup

5 Italian pork sausage links
1/4 c. onion, diced
3 cloves garlic, minced
1 t. olive oil
1 t. salt
1/4 to 1/2 t. red pepper flakes
15-oz. can diced tomatoes
32-oz. container chicken broth
2 15-oz. cans white kidney beans
4 c. spinach, torn
Garnish: grated Parmesan cheese

In a Dutch oven, sauté sausage, onion and garlic in oil until sausage is golden. Remove sausage links and slice into one-inch pieces; return to pot. Add remaining ingredients except garnish. Cover and bring to a boil. Reduce heat to low; simmer, covered, for 2 to 3 hours. Garnish with cheese. Serves 6.

Janet Parsons
Pickerington, OH

If you like pasta, cook ditalini or elbows separately and add 1/2 cup to each serving.

Grandma's Chicken Noodle Soup

16-oz. pkg. thin egg noodles,
   uncooked
1 t. oil
12 c. chicken broth
1-1/2 t. salt
1 t. poultry seasoning
1 c. celery, chopped
1 c. onion, chopped
Optional: 1 c. carrot, peeled
   and chopped
1/3 c. cornstarch
1/4 c. cold water
4 c. cooked chicken, diced

Bring a large pot of water to boil
over medium-high heat; add noodles
and oil. Cook according to package
directions; drain and set aside.
Combine broth, salt and poultry
seasoning in the same pot; bring to
a boil over medium heat. Stir in
vegetables; reduce heat, cover and
simmer for 15 minutes. Combine
cornstarch with cold water in a small
bowl; gradually add to soup, stirring
constantly. Stir in chicken and
noodles; heat through, about 5 to
10 minutes. Serves 8.

Evelyn Belcher
Monroeton, PA

My daughter gave me this
recipe years ago...now it's
my favorite!

33

Hungarian Mushroom Soup

1/4 c. onion, diced
8 c. sliced mushrooms
1 c. butter
1 c. all-purpose flour
2 16-oz. cans chicken broth
3 T. paprika
1/4 c. soy sauce
16-oz. container sour cream
1 T. dried parsley
1 T. dill weed
2 T. lemon juice
12-oz. can evaporated milk

In a stockpot over medium heat, sauté onion and mushrooms in butter, until tender. Stir in flour. Add remaining ingredients except evaporated milk; bring to a simmer. Stir in evaporated milk. Cover and simmer about one hour. Makes 8 to 10 servings.

Carleen Pettit
Sidney, OH

My family loves this creamy dish. It's so different from the typical soup.

Spicy Vegetable Soup

2 T. olive oil
2 onions, sliced
2 cloves garlic, minced
6 c. vegetable broth
1 c. celery, chopped
1 c. cauliflower flowerets
1 c. broccoli flowerets
1-1/2 c. green beans, sliced
4-oz. can diced green chiles
2 T. chili powder
1 T. dried oregano
1 T. ground cumin
1 t. paprika
1 t. ground sage

35

Heat oil in a large skillet over medium-high heat. Add onions and garlic; sauté until onions are tender, about 5 minutes. Transfer to a slow cooker. Add remaining ingredients, stirring to combine. Cover and cook on low setting for 6 to 7 hours. Makes 8 servings.

Sonya Labbe
Los Angeles, CA

When my vegetarian friend from New Mexico comes to visit, I'll make this slow-cooker recipe so I can spend more time with her!

Mom's Creamy Chicken Chowder

4 to 6 boneless, skinless chicken
  breasts, cubed
3 c. potatoes, peeled and cubed
12 c. chicken broth
3 cubes chicken bouillon
1 c. celery, diced
1/2 c. onion, diced
1-1/2 c. carrot, peeled and grated
1/2 c. butter
12-oz. can evaporated milk
1/2 c. water
1-1/2 c. all-purpose flour

Combine chicken, potatoes, broth,
bouillon, celery, onion and carrot in
a large pot. Simmer over medium heat
until chicken is cooked and vegetables
are tender. Stir in butter until melted;
set aside. In a blender, mix milk, water
and flour until smooth; add to soup
mixture. Cook and stir until thickened.
Serves 12 to 15.

Stephanie Swensen
Mapleton, UT

Paired with homemade bread or
rolls, this is my family's
most-requested soup.

Chicken Cacciatore Soup

1 c. rotini pasta, uncooked
3 14-1/2 oz. cans vegetable
   broth, divided
1/2 lb. boneless, skinless chicken
   breasts, cut into bite-size
   pieces
30-oz. jar extra-chunky spaghetti
   sauce with mushrooms
14-1/2 oz. can stewed tomatoes,
   chopped
1 zucchini, sliced
1 onion, chopped
2 cloves garlic, chopped
1/2 t. Italian seasoning
Optional: 1 T. red wine

Cook rotini according to package directions, substituting one can broth for part of the water; drain and set aside. Combine remaining ingredients in a large saucepan. Simmer 20 to 30 minutes, until chicken is cooked through and vegetables are tender. Stir in rotini; heat through. Serves 6 to 8.

37

Kathy Unruh
Fresno, CA
Go ahead and add a couple
drops of hot pepper sauce
for those who like it spicy!

Spring Ramen Salad

3-oz. pkg. chicken-flavored
  ramen noodles
1 t. sesame oil
1/2 c. seedless grapes, halved
1/2 c. apple, cored and diced
1/4 c. pineapple, diced
2 green onions, diced
1 c. cooked chicken, cubed
1 c. Muenster cheese, cubed
1-1/2 T. lemon juice
1/8 c. canola oil
1 t. sugar
Garnish: sesame seed

Set aside seasoning packet from ramen
noodles. Cook noodles according to
package directions. Drain noodles;
rinse with cold water. In a bowl, toss
sesame oil with noodles to coat. Stir
in fruit, onions, chicken and cheese.
In a separate bowl, whisk together
lemon juice, canola oil, sugar and
1/2 teaspoon of contents of seasoning
packet. Pour over noodle mixture; toss
to coat. Garnish with sesame seed.
Cover and chill before serving. Makes
4 servings.

Lori Rosenberg
University Heights, OH
This yummy recipe is truly
made to clean out the
fridge...you can put
almost anything in it!

Asian Summer Salad

8-oz. pkg. thin spaghetti,
  uncooked and broken
  into fourths
3/4 c. carrot, peeled and cut into
  2-inch strips
3/4 c. zucchini, cut into
  2-inch strips
3/4 c. red pepper, chopped
1/3 c. green onion, sliced
3/4 lb. deli roast turkey, cut
  into 2-inch-long strips
Garnish: chopped peanuts,
  chopped fresh cilantro

Cook pasta according to package
directions; drain and rinse with
cold water. In a bowl, combine all
ingredients except garnish. Toss with
Ginger Dressing. Refrigerate one
hour; garnish as desired. Makes
6 to 8 servings.

Ginger Dressing:

1/4 c. canola oil
3 T. rice vinegar
3 T. reduced-sodium soy sauce
2 t. sugar
1/8 t. fresh ginger, grated
1/8 t. cayenne pepper
1 clove garlic, chopped

Whisk together all ingredients.

39

Rhonda Schmidt
Emporia, KS

This salad is great in
the summertime when you
have ripe zucchini from
your garden. It is cool
and refreshing!

Panzanella Salad

1/2 loaf Italian or French bread,
   cubed
1/4 c. olive oil
salt and pepper to taste
1 red pepper, chopped
1 yellow pepper, chopped
1 orange pepper, chopped
1 cucumber, chopped
1 red onion, chopped
1 pt. cherry or grape tomatoes
1 to 2 T. capers
6 leaves fresh basil, cut into long,
   thin strips
3/4 c. vinaigrette or Italian salad
   dressing

In a bowl, toss together bread, olive oil, salt and pepper. Spread on an ungreased baking sheet and bake at 350 degrees for 5 minutes, or until golden and crisp; let cool. In a bowl, combine remaining ingredients. Just before serving, add bread cubes and toss to coat. Makes 6 to 8 servings.

Denise Herr
Galloway, OH

I've made this several times. It's a beautiful summer presentation salad and SO delicious. Garden veggies are best but absolutely not necessary!

Tarragon Steak Dinner Salad

6 c. Boston lettuce
2 pears, peeled, cored and sliced
1/2 red onion, thinly sliced
1/2 lb. grilled beef steak, thinly
    sliced
1/4 c. crumbled blue cheese
1/2 c. red wine vinaigrette salad
    dressing
1 T. fresh tarragon, minced
1/4 t. pepper

Arrange lettuce, pears and onion
on 4 serving plates. Top with sliced
steak and sprinkle with cheese.
Combine dressing, tarragon and
pepper in a small bowl; whisk well.
Drizzle dressing mixture over salad.
Serves 4.

Amanda Dixon
Dublin, OH

Delicious...a perfect
light summer meal.

Emily's Frozen Fruit Salad

16-oz. can apricot halves
20-oz. can crushed pineapple
10-oz. pkg. frozen strawberries,
    thawed
6-oz. can frozen orange juice
    concentrate, thawed
1/2 c. water
1/2 c. sugar
3 bananas, sliced

Combine undrained apricots and
pineapple. Mix in remaining
ingredients except bananas; set aside.
Arrange bananas in a 13"x9" baking
pan; pour fruit mixture over top.
Cover and freeze for at least 24 hours.
Before serving, let stand at room
temperature for about 15 minutes.
Cut into squares to serve. Makes 10 to
12 servings.

Emily Hauschild
Hutchinson, KS
The best frozen fruit salad
I've ever eaten! Years ago
when I was in 4-H, I won
a purple ribbon with
this recipe.

Spinach & Clementine Salad

2 lbs. clementines, peeled and
  sectioned
2 16-oz. pkgs. baby spinach
4 stalks celery, thinly sliced on
  the diagonal
1 c. red onion, thinly sliced
1/2 c. pine nuts or walnuts,
  toasted
1/4 c. dried cherries
2 T. red wine vinegar
1/4 c. olive oil
1 t. Dijon mustard
1 clove garlic, minced
1/8 t. sugar
salt and pepper to taste

In a large salad bowl, combine
clementines, spinach, celery, onion,
nuts and cherries. Toss to mix well.
Whisk together remaining ingredients
in a small bowl; drizzle over salad.
Serve immediately. Makes 8 servings.

43

Sharon Jones
Oklahoma City, OK

This fresh, crunchy salad
is a perfect way to use
a Christmas gift box
of clementines.

Skillet-Toasted Corn Salad

1/3 c. plus 1 T. olive oil, divided
1/3 c. lemon juice
1 T. Worcestershire sauce
3 to 4 dashes hot pepper sauce
3 cloves garlic, minced
1/4 t. salt
1/2 t. pepper
6 ears sweet corn, husked and
    kernels removed
4 red, yellow and/or green
    peppers, coarsely chopped
1/2 c. shredded Parmesan cheese
1 head romaine lettuce, cut
    crosswise into 1-inch pieces

In a jar with a tight-fitting lid, combine 1/3 cup oil, lemon juice, sauces, garlic, salt and pepper. Cover and shake well; set aside. Heat remaining oil in a large skillet over medium-high heat. Add corn; sauté for 5 minutes, or until corn is tender and golden, stirring often. Remove from heat; keep warm. Combine corn, peppers and cheese in a large bowl. Pour olive oil mixture over top; toss lightly to coat. Serve over lettuce. Makes 6 to 8 servings.

Sherri Cooper
Armada, MI

Whenever my father comes to visit, he always requests this salad. He usually stops by the local vegetable stand on his way and picks up fresh ears of corn...just for this salad!

Mustard & Thyme Potato Salad

2 baking potatoes
1 to 2 T. red wine vinegar,
    divided
1 c. mayonnaise
2 T. plus 2 t. Dijon mustard
1 t. fresh thyme, minced, or
    1/2 t. dried thyme
pepper to taste
Garnish: 2 sprigs fresh thyme

Pierce potatoes with a fork; bake at
400 degrees for 45 minutes, or until
tender. When still warm but cool
enough to handle, remove and
discard skins. Cut into bite-size
pieces. Transfer potatoes to a
medium glass bowl. While potatoes
are still warm, lightly drizzle with
vinegar. Fold potatoes over and
lightly drizzle again. Gently fold once
more; set aside. In a small bowl,
combine mayonnaise, mustard,
thyme and pepper. Pour over
potatoes. Fold until evenly coated.
Transfer to a serving bowl; garnish
with thyme. Serve warm or chilled.
Serves 4 to 6.

45

Cinde Shields
Issaquah, WA

One creamy bite of potato
salad brings back cherished
memories of family reunions
in the park, summertime pool
parties and my grandmother's
busy kitchen.

Sunny Quinoa Salad

2 c. quinoa, uncooked
2-1/2 c. chicken broth
4 green onions, thinly sliced
1/2 c. golden raisins, chopped
2 T. rice vinegar
1/2 c. orange juice
1 t. orange zest
2 T. olive oil
1/4 t. ground cumin
1 cucumber, peeled and chopped
1/2 c. fresh flat-leaf parsley,
    chopped
salt and pepper to taste

Rinse quinoa under cold water until water runs clear. In a saucepan, bring chicken broth to a boil. Add quinoa; return to a boil. Cover and simmer until quinoa has fully expanded, about 20 to 25 minutes. Remove from heat; fluff with a fork. In a large bowl, combine quinoa and remaining ingredients; mix well. Cover and chill before serving. Serves 6 to 8.

Jo Ann
With its bright flavors, this good-for-you salad makes a yummy lunch!

White Bean & Tomato Salad

15-oz. can cannellini beans,
   drained and rinsed
2 zucchini or yellow squash,
   diced
1 pt. cherry tomatoes, halved
1/2 c. red onion, chopped
3 T. olive oil
2 T. lemon juice
1/4 c. fresh cilantro, chopped

Combine all ingredients in a large
bowl. Cover and refrigerate. Let
stand at room temperature 20 to
30 minutes before serving.
Makes 6 servings.

47

Denise Neal
Castle Rock, CO
I got this delicious recipe
while on vacation in England.
We love it! If you can't get
cannellini beans, navy beans
will work fine.

A Little Different Macaroni Salad

16-oz. pkg. elbow macaroni,
  cooked
4 carrots, peeled and grated
1 sweet onion, chopped
1/2 c. red pepper, chopped
1/2 c. green pepper, chopped
2 c. mayonnaise
14-oz. can sweetened condensed
  milk
1/4 to 1/2 c. sugar
1/2 c. white vinegar
salt and pepper to taste

Combine macaroni, carrots, onion and peppers in a large bowl. In a separate bowl, whisk together mayonnaise, condensed milk, sugar and vinegar. Pour over macaroni and vegetables. Season with salt and pepper. Chill at least 8 hours to allow dressing to thicken. Mix well before serving. Makes 8 to 10 servings.

Wanda Wilson
Hamilton, GA

Sweetened condensed milk
is the secret ingredient!

Spicy Cabbage-Apple Slaw

2 c. shredded green and red
   cabbage mix
2 c. Red Delicious apples, cored
   and chopped
1/2 c. celery, chopped
2 T. walnuts, chopped and
   toasted
2 T. golden raisins
1/2 c. plain yogurt
2 T. apple juice
1 T. honey
1/2 t. cinnamon

In a large serving bowl, combine cabbage mix, apples, celery, nuts and raisins; toss well. Combine remaining ingredients in a small bowl, stirring well. Pour yogurt mixture over cabbage mixture; toss well. Cover and chill for at least 30 minutes before serving. Makes 8 servings.

49

Edie DeSpain
Logan, UT
We really like the crunchiness of this salad that comes from the cabbage, apples, celery and walnuts... yum! It goes well with pork dishes.

German Green Beans

2 14-1/2 oz. cans green beans,
   drained
15-1/4 oz. can corn, drained
1 t. seasoned salt
1 T. onion powder
1 clove garlic, minced
1 T. vinegar
4 to 5 T. olive oil
4 to 5 carrots, peeled and grated
1/2 t. dill weed
1/2 t. dried oregano
1/4 t. dried tarragon
5 slices bacon, crisply cooked
   and crumbled

In a large serving bowl, mix together
all ingredients except bacon. Cover
and refrigerate overnight, stirring
occasionally. Top with bacon and
serve at room temperature. Makes 4 to
6 servings.

Patricia Taylor
Wellsville, PA

My family loves this
so much, there's never
any left over!

Hot & Sweet Coleslaw

8 c. green cabbage, shredded
1 c. red cabbage, shredded
4 carrots, peeled and shredded
1 yellow onion, grated
1/2 c. low-fat mayonnaise
2 T. mustard
2 t. cider vinegar
1/4 c. sugar
1 t. pepper
1/4 t. cayenne pepper
Optional: salt and additional
　　pepper to taste

In a large bowl, toss together vegetables. In a separate bowl, whisk together mayonnaise, mustard, vinegar, sugar and peppers. Toss mayonnaise mixture with cabbage mixture; season with salt and additional pepper, if desired. Cover and refrigerate overnight before serving. Makes 10 to 12 servings.

51

**Karen Christiansen
Glenview, IL**

My husband, who doesn't care for salads with a lot of mayonnaise, enjoys this slaw along with pulled pork sandwiches.

Fruit Harvest Salad

32-oz. container vanilla yogurt
8-oz. pkg. cream cheese, softened
1/2 c. sugar
1/4 c. plus 1/3 c. brown sugar,
    packed and divided
1 t. vanilla extract
1 lb. seedless green grapes
1 lb. seedless red grapes
2 Gala apples, cored and diced
2 Granny Smith apples, cored
    and diced
1/2 c. sliced almonds
1/3 c. sweetened dried cranberries
15-oz. can mandarin oranges,
    drained
Optional: whipped cream

In a blender on medium speed, mix yogurt and cream cheese until smooth. Pour mixture into a large bowl. Stir in sugar, 1/4 cup brown sugar and vanilla. Add grapes, apples and almonds; toss until coated. Cover and refrigerate one hour. Uncover and smooth top of salad. Top with cranberries, oranges and whipped cream, if using. Sprinkle with remaining brown sugar. Makes 15 to 20 servings.

Shanna Painter
Alberta, Canada

I love making this salad with my young daughter. Those who watch their sugar will be happy to know calorie-free sweeteners work just as well!

Chicken & Rice Salad

3 T. red wine vinegar
1-1/2 T. extra-virgin olive oil
1/4 t. pepper
1 clove garlic, minced
2 c. long-grain rice, cooked
1-1/2 c. cooked chicken breast,
   diced
1/2 c. jarred roasted red peppers,
   drained and diced
1/2 c. Kalamata olives, pitted
   and halved
1/4 c. fresh chives, chopped
1/4 c. fresh basil, chopped
1/4 c. fresh oregano, chopped
14-oz. can artichokes, drained
   and diced
4-oz. pkg. crumbled feta cheese

In a small bowl, whisk together
vinegar, olive oil, pepper and garlic.
Set aside. In a separate bowl,
combine rice and remaining
ingredients except cheese. At serving
time, drizzle vinegar mixture over
salad; sprinkle with cheese. Makes
4 servings.

53

Francie Stutzman
N. Ft. Myers, FL

This dish is
scrumptious...I hope
you'll try it!

Roasted Veggie Tortellini Salad

20-oz. pkg. refrigerated 6-cheese
   tortellini pasta
1 red pepper, thinly sliced
3/4 c. red onion, thinly sliced
1/2 lb. asparagus, trimmed and
   cut into 1-1/2 inch pieces
salt and pepper to taste
2 T. olive oil, divided
1 zucchini, diced
7-oz. container basil pesto

Cook pasta according to package
directions; drain, rinse with cold water
and set aside. In a bowl, combine red
pepper, onion and asparagus. Season
with salt and pepper and toss with one
tablespoon olive oil. Arrange red
pepper mixture in a single layer on a
baking sheet. Bake at 450 degrees for
10 to 12 minutes. Remove from baking
sheet and set aside. Season zucchini
with salt and pepper; toss with
remaining olive oil. Arrange in a single
layer on a baking sheet. Bake for 5 to
7 minutes, until tender but not brown.
Combine roasted vegetables, cooked
tortellini and pesto in a large bowl.
Chill for at least one hour; serve
chilled. Makes 8 servings.

Christy Cox
Bristow, VA

This is a must for any
gathering! Look for the
tortellini and pesto in
the dairy or refrigerated
Italian food case.

11-Layer Garden in a Bowl

3 c. mayonnaise
2/3 c. sugar
2 10-oz. pkgs. mixed salad
   greens
1 lb. bacon, crisply cooked and
   crumbled
1 red onion, diced
10-oz. pkg. frozen peas, thawed
1 green pepper, diced
2 c. cauliflower flowerets
2 c. broccoli flowerets
1 c. sliced mushrooms
1 c. shredded Cheddar cheese
1 c. cherry tomatoes, halved
1 T. Italian seasoning

In a bowl, mix mayonnaise and
sugar until blended; set aside. Layer
half the salad greens in a large serving
bowl or 13"x9" glass baking pan.
Layer with half the mayonnaise
mixture, half the remaining
ingredients except tomatoes and
seasoning. Repeat layers. Top with
tomatoes and sprinkle with
seasoning. Cover and refrigerate
2 hours before serving. Makes
8 servings.

55

Nola Coons
Gooseberry Patch

This farm-fresh salad is for
those occasions when seven
layers just won't do!

Shrimp Tossed Salad

1 head lettuce, torn
9-oz. pkg. baby spinach
3 c. coleslaw mix
8-oz. can sliced water chestnuts, drained
1/4 to 1/2 c. golden raisins
1/4 to 1/2 c. sweetened dried cranberries
1/2 red pepper, very thinly sliced
2-lb. pkg. frozen cooked shrimp, thawed
1 carrot, peeled
1/2 c. chow mein noodles
Optional: chopped fresh dill
Garnish: sweet-and-sour salad dressing

In a large serving bowl, arrange half each of lettuce, spinach and coleslaw mix. Top with half each of water chestnuts, raisins and cranberries. Layer with remaining lettuce, spinach and coleslaw mix. Arrange red peppers around the edge of the salad. Arrange shrimp inside the pepper ring. Using a vegetable peeler, make carrot curls; arrange in center of bowl. Sprinkle with remaining water chestnuts, raisins and cranberries. Just before serving, top with chow mein noodles. If desired, sprinkle dill over the shrimp. Serve with salad dressing. Serves 6.

Amy Bleich
Jacksonville, FL
A simply scrumptious mix that's super for hot summer days!

Peppy 4-Bean Salad

14-1/2 oz. can green beans,
    drained
14-1/2 oz. can yellow beans,
    drained
15-1/2 oz. can kidney beans,
    drained
16-oz. can lima beans, drained
14-1/2 oz. can sliced carrots,
    drained
1 green pepper, chopped
1 red onion, chopped
1 c. celery, chopped
1/2 c. vinegar
1/2 c. water
1/2 c. oil
2 c. sugar
1 t. celery seed
1 t. salt

Mix together all beans and vegetables in a large bowl; set aside. In a separate bowl, whisk together remaining ingredients; toss with bean mixture. Cover and refrigerate for at least 24 hours. Makes 10 to 12 servings.

57

Debi DeVore
New Philadelphia, OH

This is my mom's recipe...
we enjoy it at all our
family cookouts.

Pasta Taco Salad

3 c. rotini pasta, uncooked
1 lb. ground beef
1-1/4 oz. pkg. taco seasoning mix
7 c. lettuce, torn
2 tomatoes, chopped
2 c. shredded Cheddar cheese
2 c. nacho-flavored tortilla chips,
   crushed

Cook pasta according to package directions; drain and rinse in cold water. Meanwhile, brown beef in a skillet; drain. Add taco seasoning and cook according to package directions. In a large bowl, combine pasta, beef and Dressing; toss until coated. Add lettuce, tomatoes and cheese. Toss to combine. Sprinkle with tortilla chips. Makes 12 to 14 servings.

Dressing:

1-1/4 c. mayonnaise
3 T. milk
3-3/4 t. cider vinegar
3-3/4 t. sugar
1 T. dry mustard

Whisk together all ingredients.

Lisa Seckora
Chippewa Falls, WI
Great at potlucks and family gatherings...everyone loves this salad with a kick!

Chilled Apple & Cheese Salad

3-oz. pkg. lemon gelatin mix
1 c. boiling water
3/4 c. cold water
2/3 c. red apple, cored and
    finely chopped
1/3 c. shredded Cheddar cheese
1/4 c. celery, chopped

In a bowl, dissolve gelatin in boiling water. Stir in cold water; chill until partially set. Fold in remaining ingredients. Pour into a 3-cup mold. Cover and chill 3 hours, or until firm. Unmold onto a serving plate. Makes 6 servings.

59

**Melody Taynor
Everett, WA**

As a girl, I was convinced that I didn't like gelatin salads. But when my Aunt Clara served this at an anniversary party, I found I had been mistaken!

Blueberry-Chicken Salad

2 c. chicken breast, cooked
  and cubed
3/4 c. celery, chopped
1/2 c. red pepper, diced
1/2 c. green onions, thinly sliced
2 c. blueberries, divided
6-oz. container lemon yogurt
3 T. mayonnaise
1/2 t. salt
Garnish: Bibb lettuce

Combine chicken and vegetables in a
large bowl. Gently stir in 1-1/2 cups
blueberries; reserve remaining berries.
In a separate bowl, blend remaining
ingredients except lettuce. Drizzle over
chicken mixture and gently toss to coat.
Cover and refrigerate 30 minutes.
Spoon salad onto lettuce-lined plates.
Top with reserved blueberries. Makes
4 servings.

Debi DeVore
New Philadelphia, OH
Fresh blueberries and lemony
yogurt add a fresh spin to
the usual chicken salad.

Pizza Salad

1 head iceberg lettuce, torn
1 c. sliced pepperoni
1 c. shredded mozzarella cheese
1 c. shredded Cheddar cheese
1 green pepper, chopped
1/2 c. sliced black olives
1/2 c. sliced mushrooms
1/2 c. red onion, sliced

Toss together all ingredients in a large bowl. Toss with Pizza Dressing at serving time. Serves 6.

Pizza Dressing:

1 c. pizza sauce
1/2 c. oil
1/4 c. red wine vinegar
1 t. sugar
1/2 t. salt
1 t. dried oregano
1/8 t. pepper
1/4 t. garlic powder

In a screw-top jar, combine all ingredients; cover and shake well.

61

Karen Curnutt
Wichita, KS
We love pizza, so I came up with this salad as a way to enjoy it in a different form. When I take it to potlucks, everyone always wants the recipe.

Black Cherry & Cranberry Salad

8-oz. can crushed pineapple
1/4 c. water
3-oz. pkg. black cherry gelatin mix
16-oz. can whole-berry cranberry
   sauce
1 c. celery, chopped
1 c. chopped walnuts
1/4 c. lemon juice

In a saucepan over medium heat, mix undrained pineapple and water. Heat to boiling; add gelatin mix and stir until gelatin is dissolved. Add remaining ingredients and stir well. Transfer to a 6-cup serving dish. Chill in refrigerator for 4 hours, or until firm. Makes 8 servings.

Leigh Ellen Eades
Summersville, WV
I remember my mother making this salad for Thanksgiving and Christmas when I was a child. Now, it's at the top of my own holiday menus!

Seafood Salad for a Crowd

3 8-oz. pkgs. cooked frozen
   shrimp, thawed
2 lbs. imitation crabmeat, cut
   into bite-size pieces
4 cucumbers, peeled and diced
6 tomatoes, diced
1 bunch green onions, chopped
1 head lettuce, chopped
4 avocados, halved, pitted
   and diced
seasoned salt with onion &
   garlic to taste
2 16-oz. pkgs. shredded
   Colby Jack cheese
Garnish: ranch salad dressing

In a large bowl, toss together all
ingredients except cheese and salad
dressing. Divide salad into individual
bowls; top with cheese and salad
dressing. Serves 15.

63

Viola Travis
Donaldson, AR

I always set aside a
container of this refreshing
salad for my father...he
gets mad if I don't!

Layered Caribbean Chicken Salad

3 c. romaine lettuce, shredded
2 c. cooked chicken, cubed
1 c. shredded Monterey Jack cheese
15-1/2 oz. can black beans, drained
    and rinsed
1-1/2 c. mango, halved, pitted
    and cubed
1/2 c. plum tomatoes, chopped
1 c. shredded Cheddar cheese
1/2 c. green onions, thinly sliced
1/2 c. cashews, chopped

In a large clear glass serving bowl, layer all salad ingredients in order listed, except cashews. Spoon Dressing evenly over salad; sprinkle cashews over top. Makes 6 servings.

Dressing:

6-oz. container piña colada yogurt
2 T. lime juice
1 t. Caribbean jerk seasoning

In a small bowl, mix all ingredients together until well blended.

Laurel Perry
Loganville, GA

This is a wonderful way to use rotisserie chicken from the deli. You won't believe how yummy the dressing is!

Lucy's Sausage Salad

14-oz. pkg. mini smoked beef
   sausages, divided
1 t. canola oil
1 c. corn
15-1/2 oz. can black beans,
   drained and rinsed
1 T. canned jalapeño pepper,
   seeded and minced
1 c. red pepper, chopped
Garnish: fresh cilantro sprigs

Measure out half the sausages; set
aside for a future use. Slice
remaining sausages into 3 pieces
each. In a skillet, sauté sausages in
oil over medium heat until lightly
golden; drain. In a large bowl,
combine corn, beans, jalapeño and
red pepper. Stir in sausage. Toss with
Dressing; garnish with cilantro.
Serves 4.

Dressing:
3 T. low-fat plain yogurt
3 T. low-fat sour cream
1/4 c. picante sauce
1/2 c. fresh cilantro, chopped
salt and pepper to taste

Whisk together all ingredients.

Lucy Davis
Colorado Springs, CO
This deliciously different
salad may be made ahead and
chilled for one to two hours,
or served immediately.

Raspberry & Chicken Salad

1 c. white wine or chicken broth
1 c. water
4 boneless, skinless chicken breasts
1/3 c. olive oil
3 T. raspberry vinegar
1/2 t. Dijon mustard
salt and pepper to taste
10-oz. pkg. mixed salad greens
1 pt. raspberries

Combine wine or chicken broth and water in a saucepan over medium heat. Cover; bring to a boil. Reduce heat and add chicken. Cover and simmer 10 minutes, or until cooked through; drain. Let chicken cool and cut into 1/4-inch slices. Combine olive oil, vinegar, mustard, salt and pepper in a small screw-top jar; shake well. In a large bowl, toss salad greens with 1/3 of dressing. In a blender, blend 1/3 cup of raspberries and remaining dressing until smooth. Arrange salad on individual serving plates; top with chicken and remaining raspberries. Drizzle with dressing; serve immediately. Serves 4.

Rogene Rogers
Bemidji, MN

We can't wait for raspberry season so we can pick basketfuls ourselves! I like to serve this salad with fresh-baked muffins.

Lemon-Dill Chopped Salad

2 romaine lettuce hearts,
   chopped
1 c. cherry tomatoes, quartered
1 cucumber, peeled and cubed
3/4 c. baby carrots, cut in
   1/4-inch coins
1/2 c. crumbled feta cheese

In a large bowl, combine lettuce,
tomatoes, cucumber, carrots and
cheese. Cover and refrigerate. To
serve, toss with Dressing. Serves 4.

Dressing:
juice of 1 lemon
2 T. white wine vinegar
1 T. honey
2 T. fresh dill, chopped
1/4 t. salt
1/8 t. pepper
1/3 c. olive oil
1 apple, cored and coarsely
   grated

Whisk together lemon juice, vinegar,
honey, dill, salt and pepper. Slowly
whisk in oil in a thin stream; stir in
apple. Cover and refrigerate at least
2 hours.

Shirl Parsons
Cape Carteret, NC
This wonderful side dish
recipe was given to me by
a dear friend.

Scrumptious Chicken Sandwiches

1 egg, beaten
1 c. milk
4 to 6 boneless, skinless chicken
 breasts
1 c. all-purpose flour
2-1/2 T. powdered sugar
1 T. kosher salt
1/2 t. pepper
Optional: 1/8 t. allspice
oil for frying
4 to 6 hamburger buns, split
 and lightly toasted
Garnish: mayonnaise, dill
 pickle slices

Mix egg and milk together in an
11"x7" baking pan. Place chicken in
pan, turn to coat and refrigerate for
one hour. In a bowl, combine flour,
sugar and spices. In a heavy skillet,
heat one inch of oil to 400 degrees.
Working in batches of 3, drain chicken,
reserving egg mixture, and lightly
dredge in flour mixture. Dip back into
egg mixture, then into flour mixture
again. Place very carefully into hot oil.
Fry for 8 to 10 minutes, until done on
both sides and juices run clear. Drain
chicken on a wire rack. Assemble
sandwiches on toasted buns and garnish
as desired. Makes 4 to 6.

Sandy Carpenter
Washington, WV
These taste so much like
a popular restaurant's
sandwiches but cost
much less!

Scott's Ham & Pear Sandwiches

8 slices sourdough bread
4 slices Swiss cheese
1-1/4 lbs. sliced deli ham
15-oz. can pear halves, drained
　and thinly sliced

Spread each bread slice with a thin
layer of Spiced Butter. On each of
4 slices, place one slice of cheese;
layer evenly with ham and pears.
Top with remaining bread slices and
press together gently. Spread the
outside of the sandwiches with
Spiced Butter. Heat a large skillet
over medium-high heat and cook
until crisp and golden, about
5 minutes on each side. Makes
4 sandwiches.

Spiced Butter:

1 c. butter, softened
2 t. pumpkin pie spice
1 t. ground coriander
1 t. ground ginger
1 t. salt

Combine all ingredients until
smooth and evenly mixed.

Kathy Majeske
Denver, PA

My brother, who is an amazing
cook, gave me this recipe.
The spiced butter makes it
especially crispy and good!

Tuna Panini

12-oz. can tuna, drained
1 onion, chopped
4 to 6 dill pickle spears, chopped
1/2 to 3/4 c. carrot, peeled,
  shredded and chopped
3/4 to 1 c. shredded mozzarella
  cheese
mayonnaise to taste
1 T. olive oil
8 slices multi-grain bread, toasted
1 tomato, sliced

In a bowl, mix tuna, onion, pickles, carrot, cheese and mayonnaise. In a panini press or skillet, heat olive oil over medium heat until hot. For each sandwich, top one slice of toasted bread with tuna mixture, 2 slices of tomato and second slice of bread. Place sandwich in a panini press or skillet; heat one to 2 minutes, or until cheese is melted. Makes 4 sandwiches.

Mary Stratton
Abington, MA

This is a quick recipe that's perfect whenever time is short and tummies are rumbling!

Louisiana Sausage Sandwiches

19.76-oz. pkg. Italian pork
   sausage links
1 green pepper, sliced into
   bite-size pieces
1 onion, sliced into bite-size
   pieces
8-oz. can tomato sauce
1/8 t. pepper
6 hoagie rolls, split

In a large skillet, brown sausage links
over medium heat. Cut into 1/2-inch
slices; place in a slow cooker. Stir in
remaining ingredients except rolls.
Cover and cook on low setting for
8 hours. Spoon into rolls with a
slotted spoon. Makes 6 sandwiches.

71

Dana Cunningham
Lafayette, LA

After working the county fair
one year with a friend, I
learned how to make these
sandwiches like a pro!

Baked Filled Sandwiches

1 loaf frozen bread dough, thawed
2 T. mayonnaise-type salad
 dressing
1/2 T. dried, minced onion
3/4 t. Italian seasoning
8 slices Swiss cheese
10 slices deli honey ham
10 slices deli roast turkey
1 egg, beaten
1 t. water
Garnish: sesame seed

On a floured surface, roll dough into a 14-inch by 12-inch rectangle. Spread with salad dressing; sprinkle with onion and seasoning. Make ten, 1-1/2 inch cuts on each long edge of the dough. Layer dough alternately with cheese, ham and turkey, ending with turkey. Criss-cross the cut strips over the top of the meat; place on an ungreased baking sheet and set aside. Combine egg and water; brush over dough. Sprinkle with sesame seed; let rise for 30 minutes. Bake at 350 degrees for 45 minutes to one hour, until golden. Slice to serve. Serves 8.

Elaine Wilcox
Austin, MN

This recipe was a customer favorite at the Gingerbread House, the restaurant my sister and I owned together.

BBQ Chicken Calzones

12-oz. tube refrigerated
    pizza dough
3 c. cooked chicken, diced
1 c. barbecue sauce
1 c. shredded mozzarella cheese
1 egg, beaten
1 t. water

On a floured surface, roll dough
to 1/2-inch thickness; cut into
2 rectangles and place on ungreased
baking sheets. In a bowl, combine
chicken and barbecue sauce. For
each calzone, spoon half the chicken
mixture onto one half of the dough.
Top with half the cheese. Fold over
dough and seal the edges. Mix
together egg and water. Use a pastry
brush to brush egg mixture over each
calzone; use a knife to cut 3 slits in
the tops. Bake at 400 degrees for
25 minutes, or until golden.
Makes 4 servings.

73

Jill Ross
Gooseberry Patch

With a recipe this easy,
it's a pleasure to have
my children lend a hand
in the kitchen!

Grilled Chicken & Zucchini Wraps

4 boneless, skinless chicken breasts
4 to 6 zucchini, sliced lengthwise
   into 1/4-inch thick slices
olive oil
salt and pepper to taste
1/2 c. ranch salad dressing, divided
8 10-inch whole-grain flour
   tortillas
8 leaves lettuce
Garnish: shredded Cheddar cheese

Brush chicken and zucchini with olive oil; sprinkle with salt and pepper. Grill chicken over medium-high heat for 5 minutes. Turn chicken over; add zucchini to grill. Grill 5 minutes longer, or until chicken juices run clear and zucchini is tender. Slice chicken into strips; set aside. For each wrap, spread one tablespoon salad dressing on a tortilla. Top with a lettuce leaf, 1/2 cup chicken and 3 to 4 slices of zucchini. Sprinkle with cheese; roll up. Makes 8 servings.

Teresa Willett
Ontario, Canada

These wraps are a huge hit with my family...even my son who claims he doesn't like zucchini!

The Ultimate Shrimp Sandwich

3/4 lb. cooked shrimp, chopped
1/4 c. green pepper, chopped
1/4 c. celery, chopped
1/4 c. cucumber, chopped
1/4 c. tomato, diced
1/4 c. green onion, chopped
1/4 c. mayonnaise
Optional: hot pepper sauce
   to taste
6 split-top rolls, split and
   lightly toasted
2 T. butter, softened
1 c. lettuce, shredded

In a bowl, combine shrimp,
vegetables and mayonnaise; toss well.
Set aside. Spread rolls evenly with
butter; divide lettuce among rolls.
Top with shrimp mixture. Serves 6.

75

Karen Pilcher
Burleson, TX

Treat your family to this
scrumptious recipe. It also
makes a satisfying appetizer
when served on crackers.

Chicken Quesadillas El Grande

3 to 4-lb. deli roast chicken,
   shredded
3 T. salsa
salt and pepper to taste
1 onion, cut into strips
1 green pepper, cut into strips
3 T. olive oil
15-oz. can refried beans
8 10-inch flour tortillas
6-oz. pkg. shredded
   Mexican-blend cheese
Garnish: shredded lettuce, diced
   tomatoes, diced red onion,
   sour cream, guacamole,
   additional salsa

In a bowl, stir together chicken, salsa, salt and pepper; set aside. In a skillet over medium heat, cook onion and pepper in oil until crisp-tender; remove to a bowl. Evenly spread refried beans onto 4 tortillas. For each quesadilla, place one tortilla, bean-side up, in a skillet coated with non-stick vegetable spray. Top with a quarter of chicken, onion mixture and cheese. Place a plain tortilla on top. Cook over medium heat until layers start to warm, about 2 minutes. Flip over and cook until tortilla is crisp and filling is hot. Cut each quesadilla into wedges and garnish as desired. Serves 4.

Michelle Papp
Rutherford, NJ
I just whipped this up
one afternoon for a quick
lunch and it was a
hit...so satisfying!

Buffalo Chicken Sandwich

6 boneless chicken breasts
1 onion, chopped
6 stalks celery, chopped
2 to 3 T. olive oil
1/2 c. all-purpose flour
Optional: 1 t. seasoning salt
17-1/2 oz. bottle buffalo
   wing sauce
6 soft buns, split
Garnish: ranch or blue cheese
   salad dressing, crumbled blue
   cheese, additional wing sauce

Flatten chicken breasts to 1/4-inch thin between pieces of wax paper; set aside. In a skillet over medium-low heat, sauté onion and celery in oil until tender. In a shallow bowl, combine flour and seasoning salt, if using. Dredge chicken pieces in flour mixture. Add chicken on top of onion mixture in pan. Cook for 5 minutes; flip chicken and cook an additional 5 minutes. Add buffalo wing sauce to pan. Cover; increase heat to medium, and cook 5 to 7 minutes, until chicken juices run clear. Serve on buns; garnish as desired. Makes 6 sandwiches.

Susan Buetow
Du Quoin, IL

Besides looking tasty, this sandwich is very easy to make. It's my go-to recipe when hubby is having buddies over!

Cheesy Zucchini Joes

2 T. butter
2 zucchini, halved and sliced
1/8 t. red pepper flakes
1/8 t. garlic powder
salt and pepper to taste
1 c. marinara or spaghetti sauce
1 to 2 c. shredded mozzarella
   cheese
4 6-inch sub rolls, split

Melt butter in a skillet over medium heat. Fry zucchini in butter until golden and slightly tender. Add seasonings. Stir in sauce. Cook and stir until sauce is heated through. For each sandwich, spoon a generous amount of zucchini mixture onto bottom half of bun. Sprinkle with cheese and replace bun top. Wrap sandwiches individually in aluminum foil. Place on a baking sheet and bake at 350 degrees for 15 minutes, or until heated through and cheese is melted. Makes 4 sandwiches.

Kim McLaughlin
Cambridge, OH

My grandma planted lots of zucchini. We always joked that she would serve zucchini in every dish possible!

Game-Day Sandwich

3 T. mayonnaise
1 T. mustard
1-lb. round loaf Hawaiian-style
   bread
1/4 lb. sliced deli turkey
1/4 lb. sliced deli roast beef
3 slices Swiss cheese
3 lettuce leaves
1/4 lb. sliced deli ham
6 slices bacon, crisply cooked
3 slices Cheddar cheese
6 slices tomato

Mix mayonnaise and mustard together. Cut bread horizontally into 3 layers. Spread half of mayonnaise mixture on the bottom layer. Add turkey, roast beef, Swiss cheese and lettuce. Cover with middle bread layer; spread with remaining mayonnaise mixture. Add ham, bacon, Cheddar cheese and tomato. Top with remaining bread layer. Cut into 6 to 8 slices. Makes 6 to 8 servings.

Yvonne Coleman
Statesville, NC
My husband loves this sandwich and requests it on his birthday. It has something to please everyone.

79

Backyard Big South-of-the-Border Burgers

4-oz. can chopped green chiles, drained
1/4 c. picante sauce
12 round buttery crackers, crushed
4-1/2 t. chili powder
1 T. ground cumin
1/2 t. smoke-flavored cooking sauce
1/2 t. salt
1/2 t. pepper
2 lbs. lean ground beef
1/2 lb. ground pork sausage
6 slices Pepper Jack cheese
6 sesame seed hamburger buns, split
Garnish: lettuce leaves, sliced tomato

In a large bowl, combine first 8 ingredients. Crumble beef and sausage over mixture and mix well. Form into 6 patties. Grill, covered, over medium heat for 5 to 7 minutes on each side, or until no longer pink. Top with cheese. Grill until cheese is melted. Grill buns, cut-side down, for one to 2 minutes, or until toasted. Serve burgers on buns, garnished as desired. Makes 6 servings.

Paula Marchesi
Lenhartsville, PA

Every time I bite into a scrumptious, juicy burger cooked on an outside grill, I'm a kid again, at our picnic table with family & friends.

Seaside Salmon Buns

14-oz. can salmon, drained
  and flaked
1/4 c. green pepper, chopped
1 T. onion, chopped
2 t. lemon juice
1/2 c. mayonnaise
6 hamburger buns, split
1/2 c. shredded Cheddar cheese
6 thick tomato slices

Mix salmon, pepper, onion, lemon juice and mayonnaise. Pile salmon mixture onto bottom bun halves; sprinkle with cheese. Arrange salmon-topped buns on an ungreased baking sheet. Broil until lightly golden and cheese is melted. Top with tomato slices and remaining bun halves. Serves 6.

81

Sharon Velenosi
Garden Grove, CA

For a real homestyle treat, substitute fresh-baked biscuits for the hamburger buns.

Texas Steak Sandwiches

8 slices frozen Texas toast
1-1/2 lbs. deli roast beef, sliced
steak sauce to taste
8 slices provolone cheese
Optional: sliced green pepper and
red onion, sautéed

Bake Texas toast on a baking sheet at
425 degrees for about 5 minutes per
side, until softened and lightly golden;
set aside. Warm roast beef in a skillet
over medium heat until most of the
juices have evaporated; stir in steak
sauce. Divide beef evenly among 4 toast
slices; top with cheese, pepper and
onion, if desired. Place beef-topped
toast and remaining toast on a baking
sheet; bake at 425 degrees until
cheese is melted. Combine to form
sandwiches. Makes 4 sandwiches.

Julie Horn
Chrisney, IN

My husband and I love these
hearty sandwiches. They're
super simple to make...when
guests drop by, I can whip
them up in no time.

Mexican Hot Dogs

8 hot dogs
8 slices bacon
8 hot dog buns
1 c. sour cream
1/2 c. onion, chopped
3/4 c. tomato, chopped
4-oz. can chopped jalapeño
    peppers, drained
Garnish: mustard and catsup

Pierce hot dogs with a fork 3 or
4 times. Wrap one slice of bacon
around each hot dog. Over medium
heat, grill or sauté on a griddle until
bacon is lightly golden on all sides.
Remove wire twist from hot dog bun
bag. Microwave buns in bag for
30 to 45 seconds. Carefully remove
buns from bag; cut open buns.
Spread sour cream on both halves of
each bun. Place bacon-wrapped hot
dog in bun. Top with onion, tomato
and jalapeños. Garnish with mustard
and catsup. Makes 8.

83

**Leslie Limon
Yahualica, Mexico**

My hubby introduced me
to these unbelievably good
hot dogs. This is how
they're made in his
hometown in Mexico.

Mom's Slow-Cooker Mini Reubens

1/4 to 1/2 lb. deli corned beef, chopped
2 16-oz. pkgs. shredded Swiss cheese
8-oz. bottle Thousand Island salad dressing
32-oz. pkg. refrigerated sauerkraut, drained and chopped
Optional: 1 t. caraway seed
1 to 2 loaves party rye bread
Garnish: dill pickle slices

Put all ingredients except party rye and pickles in a slow cooker. Cover and cook on low setting for about 4 hours, or until mixture is hot and cheese is melted. Stir to blend well. To serve, arrange party rye slices and pickles on separate plates around slow cooker. Makes 10 to 12 servings.

Cheryl Breeden
North Platte, NE

This was always my mom's favorite recipe during football season...even if our team lost, dinner was always a winner!

Toasted Chicken Salad Bagels

6 c. cooked chicken, chopped
2 c. celery, chopped
1 c. almonds, chopped and
   toasted
1/4 c. lemon juice
1/4 c. onion, grated
1 t. salt
2 c. mayonnaise
1 c. shredded Cheddar cheese
12 bagels, sliced
2 c. potato chips, crushed

In a bowl, combine all ingredients
except bagels and chips. Spread
mixture on bottom halves of bagels.
Transfer bagels and tops to an
ungreased baking sheet. Broil for
3 to 5 minutes, until golden.
Sprinkle chips on chicken mixture.
Replace bagel tops. Makes
12 servings.

85

Kara McCreary
Wooster, OH

A crunchy twist on
traditional chicken
salad sandwiches.

Triple-Take Grilled Cheese

1 T. oil
8 slices sourdough bread
1/4 c. butter, softened and divided
4 slices American cheese
4 slices Muenster cheese
1/2 c. shredded sharp Cheddar
   cheese
Optional: 4 slices red onion,
   4 slices tomato, 1/4 c. chopped
   fresh basil

Heat oil in a skillet over medium
heat. Spread 2 bread slices with one
tablespoon butter; place one slice
butter-side down on skillet. Layer
one slice American, one slice Muenster
and 2 tablespoons Cheddar cheese on
bread. If desired, top with an onion
slice, a tomato slice and one tablespoon
basil. Place second buttered bread slice
on top of sandwich in skillet. Reduce
heat to medium-low. Cook until
golden on one side, about 3 to
5 minutes; flip and cook until golden
on the other side. Repeat with
remaining ingredients. Makes
4 sandwiches.

Abigail Smith
Worthington, OH

Delicious in winter with
a steaming bowl of tomato
soup. And delicious in
summer with produce fresh
from the garden!

Chicken Tacos

2 T. olive oil
1 onion, chopped
2 T. garlic, minced
2 to 3 lbs. boneless, skinless
   chicken thighs or breasts, cut
   into bite-size pieces
10-oz. can diced tomatoes with
   green chiles
4-oz. can diced green chiles
1/8 to 1/4 t. hot pepper sauce
1 T. dried cilantro
salt and pepper to taste
12-oz. pkg. 6-inch corn tortillas
Garnish: shredded Cheddar
   cheese

87

Heat oil in a large skillet over
medium heat. Sauté onion and
garlic until tender. Add chicken and
cook through. Stir in remaining
ingredients except tortillas and
cheese; reduce heat. Stirring often,
simmer 8 to 10 minutes, until most
of the liquid is cooked out. Spoon
into tortillas and garnish with cheese.
Serves 6 to 8.

Katherine Jaworowski
Devine, TX
I made up this recipe and
know it's a real winner
because it's the one dish
I never have leftovers from!

Cheeseburger Roll-Ups

2 lbs. ground beef
3/4 c. soft bread crumbs
1/2 c. onion, minced
2 eggs, beaten
1-1/2 t. salt
1-1/2 t. pepper
12-oz. pkg. shredded Cheddar
   cheese
6 to 8 sandwich buns, split
Garnish: catsup, mustard
   and lettuce

In a large bowl, combine beef, bread crumbs, onion, eggs, salt and pepper; mix well. Pat out into an 18-inch by 14-inch rectangle on a piece of wax paper. Spread cheese over meat, leaving a 3/4-inch border around edges. Roll up jelly-roll fashion starting at short edge. Press ends to seal. Place on a lightly greased 15"x10" jelly-roll pan. Bake at 350 degrees for one hour, or until internal temperature on a meat thermometer reaches 160 degrees. Let stand at least 10 minutes before slicing. Slice and serve on buns; garnish as desired. Serves 6 to 8.

Kelly Alderson
Erie, PA

Made before we leave to go camping, these super-simple sandwiches disappear just as soon as our tent is set up!

Party-Time Lasagna Buns

4 French bread rolls
1 lb. ground beef
1.35-oz. pkg. onion or
   mushroom soup mix
1/4 t. dried oregano
1/4 t. dried basil
8-oz. can tomato sauce
3/4 c. cottage cheese
2 c. shredded mozzarella cheese,
   divided
1 egg, beaten

Slice the top off each roll and set aside. Hollow out the rolls. In a skillet over medium heat, brown beef; drain. Stir in soup mix, seasonings and tomato sauce. Simmer until heated through. In a bowl, mix cottage cheese, one cup mozzarella and egg. For each sandwich, spoon a layer of the beef mixture into the bottom of a bun. Spoon on a layer of cheese mixture and a layer of beef mixture. Top with remaining mozzarella. Replace bun top and wrap in aluminum foil. Place on a baking sheet and bake at 400 degrees for 30 minutes, or until cheese is melted. Makes 4 sandwiches.

89

Joyce Stath
Tell City, IN

Here's a hint to prevent the rolls from tearing...place them in the freezer for about an hour prior to slicing.

Yiayia's Chicken Pitas

1/2 c. plain yogurt
1/4 c. cucumber, finely chopped
1/2 t. dill weed
1/4 t. dried mint, crushed
4 pita bread rounds
4 lettuce leaves
2 c. cooked chicken, cubed
1 tomato, thinly sliced
1/3 c. crumbled feta cheese

In a small bowl, stir together yogurt, cucumber, dill weed and mint; set aside. For each sandwich, layer a pita with lettuce, chicken, tomato and cheese. Spoon yogurt mixture on top. Roll up pita and secure with a wooden toothpick. Serve immediately. Makes 4 servings.

Tori Willis
Champaign, IL

Though not exactly like my grandma's famous Greek sandwiches, they're pretty darn close!

All-American Sandwiches

1-1/2 T. olive oil
2 red onions, thinly sliced
3-1/2 T. red wine vinegar
6 c. arugula leaves, divided
3/4 c. mayonnaise
salt and pepper to taste
4 ciabatta rolls, halved
3/4 lb. thinly sliced smoked
   deli turkey
3/4 c. crumbled blue cheese

Heat oil in a skillet over medium-high heat. Add onions and sauté until soft and lightly golden. Remove from heat and stir in vinegar. Set aside. Chop enough arugula to equal one cup. Stir in mayonnaise; season with salt and pepper. Spread arugula mixture over cut sides of rolls. Divide turkey evenly among bottom halves of rolls. Top with cheese, onion mixture, remaining arugula leaves and top halves of rolls. Makes 4 sandwiches.

JoAnn
Celebrate summer with these yummy sandwiches...the blue cheese is scrumptious!

Annelle's Special Veggie Melts

1 c. sliced baby portabella
   mushrooms
1/4 c. olive oil
1 loaf focaccia bread, halved
   horizontally
15-oz. jar whole roasted red
   peppers, drained
1-1/2 t. Italian seasoning
1 c. shredded Fontina cheese

In a skillet over medium heat, sauté
mushrooms in olive oil until tender.
Place bread halves on an ungreased
baking sheet. On one bread half,
layer peppers, mushrooms and Italian
seasoning. Top both halves evenly with
cheese. Broil until lightly golden.
Assemble sandwich and cut into
4 pieces. Makes 4 servings.

Amy Butcher
Columbus, GA

I'm lucky enough to live in
a neighborhood with a corner
bakery. Annelle, its owner,
makes the best focaccia
I've ever tasted!

Beef Stroganoff Sandwich

2 lbs. ground beef
1/2 c. onion, chopped
1/2 t. garlic powder
1 t. salt
1/2 t. pepper
1 loaf French bread, halved
   lengthwise
4 to 6 T. butter, softened
2 c. sour cream
2 tomatoes, diced
1 green pepper, diced
3 c. shredded Cheddar cheese

In a skillet over medium heat, brown beef and onion. Drain; stir in seasonings. Spread both halves of bread with butter; place butter-side up on an ungreased baking sheet. Remove skillet from heat; stir in sour cream. Spoon beef mixture onto bread; sprinkle with remaining ingredients. Bake at 350 degrees for 20 minutes, or until cheese is melted. If crisper bread is desired, bake a little longer. Slice into 3-inch portions to serve. Makes 6 servings.

Carol Blankenship
Hamilton, OH

My family just loves this open-face sandwich! I always make it for special occasions like family get-togethers. It's a great recipe.

Stuffed Bacon Cheeseburgers

1 lb. ground beef
1 T. garlic, minced
1 T. steak seasoning
1 T. dried parsley
1/2 t. paprika
1/2 t. onion powder
1 T. Worcestershire sauce
4 slices bacon, crisply cooked
   and cut in half
2 slices Cheddar cheese,
   cut into quarters
salt and pepper to taste
4 hamburger buns, split
Garnish: mustard, catsup,
   mayonnaise

In a bowl, mix beef, garlic, seasonings and Worcestershire sauce just until combined. Form into 8 thin patties. For each burger, place 2 pieces of bacon and 2 slices of cheese onto 4 patties. Top with another patty and seal edges. Sprinkle with salt and pepper. Grill over medium heat to desired doneness. Serve on buns, garnished as desired. Makes 4 servings.

Rebecca Reynoso
Ballwin, MO

What a wonderful surprise
to discover bacon and
cheese in the center of
a juicy burger!

Famous Hidden Sandwich

1 slice rye bread
1 slice deli ham
1 slice Swiss cheese
1 slice deli turkey
1 c. lettuce, shredded
1/2 c. Russian or Thousand
   Island salad dressing
1 egg, hard-boiled, peeled
   and sliced
2 slices tomato
2 slices bacon, crisply cooked
Garnish: sweet pickle slices

Place bread slice on a plate. Layer
with ham, cheese and turkey slices.
Mound shredded lettuce on top.
Cover with salad dressing. Top
with egg slices and tomato slices;
criss-cross bacon slices on top.
Garnish with sweet pickle slices.
Makes one sandwich.

95

Jennie Gist
Gooseberry Patch

I have fond memories of
lunching at the old
department store downtown
with my best friend. This
sandwich was a favorite...
you'll need a knife and fork!

Kentucky Hot Browns

1/4 c. butter
1/4 c. all-purpose flour
2 c. milk
2 cubes chicken bouillon
16-oz. pkg. pasteurized process
   cheese spread, cubed
6 slices bread, toasted
12 slices deli turkey
6 slices deli ham
6 slices bacon, crisply cooked
6 slices tomato

Melt butter in a heavy saucepan over low heat. Stir in flour until smooth. Cook one minute, stirring constantly. Stir in milk and bouillon cubes. Cook until thick and bubbly. Add cheese and stir until smooth. Place toast slices in a buttered 13"x9" baking pan. Layer each with turkey and ham. Evenly spread cheese sauce over ham. Top each with bacon and tomato. Bake, uncovered, at 350 degrees for 3 to 5 minutes, until bubbly. Makes 6 servings.

Angie Stone
Argillite, KY

I learned to make these cheesy-good sandwiches when I was very young. They're a real favorite here in Kentucky.

Honey-Barbecued Pork

2 to 3-lb. pork roast
2 onions, chopped
12-oz. bottle barbecue sauce
1/4 c. honey
6 to 8 sandwich rolls, split

Place pork in a slow cooker. Add onions, barbecue sauce and honey. Cover and cook on low setting for 6 to 8 hours. Use 2 forks to shred roast; mix well. Serve on rolls. Makes 6 to 8 servings.

97

Carol Smith
West Lawn, PA

This slow-cooker recipe is my mom's. Try it on mini buns for sliders!

Farmhouse Honey Mustard

1/4 c. mayonnaise
1/4 c. Dijon mustard
1/4 c. honey
1 T. mustard
1 T. white vinegar
1/8 t. paprika

Whisk together all ingredients in a small bowl. Cover and store in the refrigerator for up to one week. Makes about one cup.

Virginia Watson
Scranton, PA

There are so many ways to use this sweet-tangy mustard. You can spread it on sandwiches, drizzle over salads or spoon into a bowl for dipping chicken tenders...yum!

Bacon-Onion Croutons

6 slices French bread, crusts
   trimmed
2 T. bacon drippings
2 T. olive oil
1/2 t. onion powder
1 t. poppy seed
1/2 t. sesame seed, toasted

Cube bread; set aside. Heat
remaining ingredients in a skillet
over medium heat; stir in bread
cubes until well coated. Remove
from heat; spread mixture in a
single layer on an ungreased
15"x10" jelly-roll pan. Bake at
300 degrees until golden and crisp,
about 25 to 30 minutes. Let cool.
Store in an airtight container.
Makes about 2 cups.

99

Nancy Wise
Little Rock, AR

Why use store-bought
when homemade tastes
so much better?

Creamy Basil Salad Dressing

1 t. shallot, chopped
1 clove garlic, chopped
2/3 c. Greek yogurt
3 T. balsamic vinegar
1 T. lemon juice
3 T. olive oil
1/2 c. dried basil
salt and pepper to taste

Place all ingredients except salt and pepper in a food processor or blender. Proccess until smooth. Season with salt and pepper. Keep refrigerated. Makes about 1-1/2 cups.

Pat Minnich
El Cajon, CA

I grow my own basil and love this recipe. The dressing is so flavorful you would never guess it's low in fat!

Zesty Pita Crisps

6 T. sesame oil
1-1/2 t. ground cumin
salt to taste
3 pita rounds, split
Garnish: additional salt
    and cumin

In a small bowl, stir together oil,
cumin and salt. Brush the cut sides
of the pita rounds with oil mixture.
Cut each round into 6 triangles.
Arrange in a single layer in an
ungreased 15"x10" jelly-roll pan.
Bake at 350 degrees for 10 to
12 minutes, until golden. Toss
warm crisps with additional salt and
cumin; let cool. Serve immediately
or store in an airtight container.
Makes about 3 cups.

Brenda Smith
Delaware, OH

Oh-so simple! Pop these
in the oven while the soup
simmers on the stove and
the salad is tossed.

Refrigerator Pickles

3 c. cucumbers, peeled and sliced
1 onion, thinly sliced
3/4 c. sugar
2/3 c. white vinegar
1/2 t. celery seed
1/2 t. mustard seed
1/4 t. salt

Mix cucumbers and onion in a glass or plastic bowl; set aside. Stir remaining ingredients together in a microwave-safe container. Microwave on high for 3 minutes, stirring after 2 minutes. Pour over cucumber mixture. Cover and refrigerate for 24 hours before serving to blend flavors. Keep refrigerated. Makes one quart.

Kay Barg
Sandy, UT

Super simple...a great recipe for first-time pickle makers.

Cheese & Garlic Croutons

1/4 c. butter
1/2 t. dried oregano
1/2 t. dried basil
1/2 t. celery salt
2 cloves garlic, minced
1 T. onion, minced
2 c. whole-wheat bread, cubed
2 T. grated Parmesan cheese

Heat butter in a large skillet. Add seasonings, garlic and onion; cook for about one minute to soften. Stir in bread cubes; sauté until golden and crisp. Toss with cheese until coated. Cool; store in an airtight container. Makes 2 cups.

103

Kendall Hale
Lynn, MA

These savory croutons are delicious sprinkled in a bowl of soup or tossed in a dinner salad.

Mom's Hot Bacon Dressing

4 slices bacon
2 T. sugar
2 T. all-purpose flour
1 egg, beaten
2 T. cider vinegar
1/4 c. water
3/4 c. milk

In a skillet over medium heat, cook bacon until crisp. Remove bacon and reserve drippings in skillet. In a small bowl, mix sugar, flour, egg and vinegar until smooth. Stir in water and milk and add to drippings. Crumble bacon and return to skillet. Cook over medium-low heat until thickened. More water or milk may be added until dressing reaches desired consistency. Serve warm. Store in the refrigerator for up to one week. Makes about 2 cups.

Jacqueline Kurtz
Wernersville, PA

My mom used to make this all the time to drizzle over fresh endive...it's a country classic. This dressing is very good added to homemade hot potato salad too.

Blue Cheese Cut-Out Crackers

1 c. all-purpose flour
7 T. butter, softened
7 T. crumbled blue cheese
1/2 t. dried parsley
1 egg yolk
1/8 t. salt
4 t. whipping cream
cayenne pepper to taste

Mix all ingredients together; let rest
for 30 minutes. Roll dough out to
about 1/8-inch thick. Use small
cookie cutters to cut out crackers.
Bake on ungreased baking sheets at
400 degrees for 8 to 10 minutes,
just until golden. Let cool; remove
carefully. Store in an airtight
container. Makes 1-1/2 to 2 dozen.

105

Vickie
Delicate cheese wafers
with a touch of
hot pepper!

Lemony Sage Mayonnaise

2 c. mayonnaise
1/2 c. fresh sage, finely chopped,
   or 3 T. dried sage
2 T. lemon juice
1 T. plus 1 t. lemon zest
1 T. garlic, minced
1 t. pepper

Whisk together all ingredients. Cover and store in the refrigerator for up to one week. Makes about 2 cups.

Stacie Avner
Delaware, OH

Top sandwiches with
this spread...it's
packed with flavor!

Spicy Chili Crackers

16-oz. pkg. saltine crackers
1 c. olive oil
1-oz. pkg. ranch salad dressing
   mix
2 t. chili seasoning mix
1 t. garlic powder
Optional: cayenne pepper
   to taste

Place crackers in a large bowl;
set aside. Combine remaining
ingredients in a separate bowl and
stir to mix. Pour over crackers;
gently stir and let stand overnight.
May also be spread on a baking sheet
and baked at 250 degrees for 20 to
30 minutes. Store in an airtight
container. Makes 15 to 18 servings.

Gloria Robertson
Midland, TX
These savory crackers are
irresistible! Serve with a
bowl of soup or add to your
game-day buffet table.

INDEX

INDEX

A Little Different Macaroni Salad, page 48

Chicken Noodle Gumbo, page 8

Peppy 4-Bean Salad, page 57

Triple-Take Grilled Cheese, page 86

Our Story

Back in 1984, we were next-door neighbors raising our families in the little town of Delaware, Ohio. Two moms with small children, we were looking for a way to do what we loved and stay home with the kids too. We had always shared a love of home cooking and making memories with family & friends and so, after many a conversation over the backyard fence, **Gooseberry Patch** was born.

We put together our first catalog at our kitchen tables, enlisting the help of our loved ones wherever we could. From that very first mailing, we found an immediate connection with many of our customers and it wasn't long before we began receiving letters, photos and recipes from these new friends. In 1992, we put together our very first cookbook, compiled from hundreds of these recipes and, the rest, as they say, is history.

Hard to believe it's been over 25 years since those kitchen-table days! From that original little **Gooseberry Patch** family, we've grown to include an amazing group of creative folks who love cooking, decorating and creating as much as we do. Today, we're best known for our homestyle, family-friendly cookbooks, now recognized as national bestsellers.

Jo Ann & Vickie

One thing's for sure, we couldn't have done it without our friends all across the country. Each year, we're honored to turn thousands of your recipes into our collectible cookbooks. Our hope is that each book captures the stories and heart of all of you who have shared with us. Whether you've been with us since the beginning or are just discovering us, welcome to the **Gooseberry Patch** family!

Visit us online:
www.gooseberrypatch.com
1•800•854•6673

U.S. to Canadian Recipe Equivalents

Volume Measurements

1/4 teaspoon	1 mL
1/2 teaspoon	2 mL
1 teaspoon	5 mL
1 tablespoon = 3 teaspoons	15 mL
2 tablespoons = 1 fluid ounce	30 mL
1/4 cup	60 mL
1/3 cup	75 mL
1/2 cup = 4 fluid ounces	125 mL
1 cup = 8 fluid ounces	250 mL
2 cups = 1 pint =16 fluid ounces	500 mL
4 cups = 1 quart	1 L

Weights

1 ounce	30 g
4 ounces	120 g
8 ounces	225 g
16 ounces = 1 pound	450 g

Oven Temperatures

300° F	150° C
325° F	160° C
350° F	180° C
375° F	190° C
400° F	200° C
450° F	230° C

Baking Pan Sizes

Square

8x8x2 inches	2 L = 20x20x5 cm
9x9x2 inches	2.5 L = 23x23x5 cm

Rectangular

13x9x2 inches	3.5 L = 33x23x5 cm

Loaf

9x5x3 inches	2 L = 23x13x7 cm

Round

8x1-1/2 inches	1.2 L = 20x4 cm
9x1-1/2 inches	1.5 L = 23x4 cm

Recipe Abbreviations

t. = teaspoon	ltr. = liter
T. = tablespoon	oz. = ounce
c. = cup	lb. = pound
pt. = pint	doz. = dozen
qt. = quart	pkg. = package
gal. = gallon	env. = envelope

Kitchen Measurements

A pinch = 1/8 tablespoon	1 fluid ounce = 2 tablespoons
3 teaspoons = 1 tablespoon	4 fluid ounces = 1/2 cup
2 tablespoons = 1/8 cup	8 fluid ounces = 1 cup
4 tablespoons = 1/4 cup	16 fluid ounces = 1 pint
8 tablespoons = 1/2 cup	32 fluid ounces = 1 quart
16 tablespoons = 1 cup	16 ounces net weight = 1 pound
2 cups = 1 pint	
4 cups = 1 quart	
4 quarts = 1 gallon	